★ IT'S MY STATE! ★
Nebraska

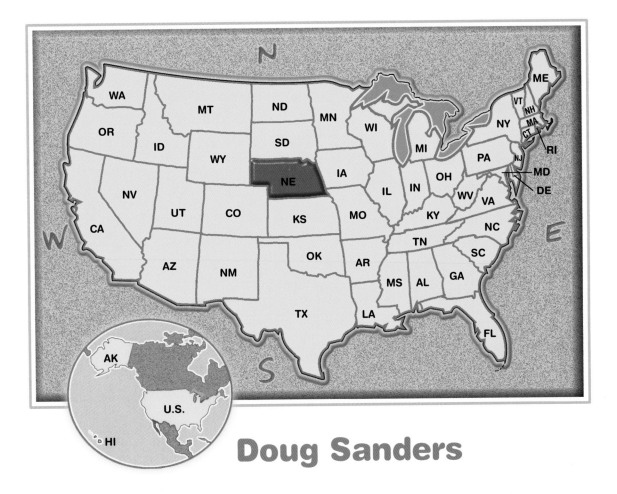

Doug Sanders

Marshall Cavendish
Benchmark
New York

Marshall Cavendish Benchmark
99 White Plains Road
Tarrytown, New York 10591-9001
www.marshallcavendish.us

Library of Congress Cataloging-in-Publication Data

Sanders, Doug, 1972-
Nebraska / by Doug Sanders.
p. cm. — (It's my state!)
Summary: "Surveys the history, geography, economy, and people of
Nebraska"—Provided by publisher.
Includes bibliographical references and index.
ISBN 0-7614-1911-X
1. Nebraska—Juvenile literature. I. Title. II. Series.
F666.3.S26   2005   978.2—dc22   2005018061

Photo research by Candlepants Incorporated

Cover photograph: Mark Andersen / Rubberball / PictureQuest

Back cover illustration: The license plate shows Nebraska's postal abbreviation followed by its year of statehood.

The photographs in this book are used by permission and through the courtesy of: *Corbis*: 41, 50, 52 (bottom), 53 (top), 73 (middle); Roy Morsch, 4 (top); David Muench, 4 (middle), 14; Tom Bean, 10, 13, 54; Jim Reed, 17; James L. Amos, 23; Connie Ricca, 31; Charles E. Rotkin, 42; Bettmann, 24, 52 (middle), 53 (bottom); Philip Gould, 67, 72 (top); Vince Streano, 69, 72 (middle); Ed Eckstein, 71; Terry Eggers, 73 (bottom). *Super Stock*: 15 (bottom), 39; Tom Algire, 15 (top); age footstock, 58. *Animals Animals / Earth Scenes*: Doug Wechsler, 4 (bottom); Leonard Rue Enterprises, 5 (top); Darren Bennett, 21 (top). *Photo Researchers, Inc.*: Tom McHugh, 5 (middle); Laurie O'Keefe, 5 (bottom); Rod Planck, 20 (top); Tim Davis, 20 (middle); Jim Zipp, 21 (middle); Francois Gohier, 21 (bottom). *Picture Quest*: Larry Mayer / Creatas, 8. *Minden Pictures*: Jim Brandenburg, 20 (bottom). *Nebraska Division of Travel and Tourism*: 9, 11, 18, 46, 48, 51, 56, 57, 64, 74. *Museum of Nebraska Art, University of Nebraska at Kearny*: 26. *Art Resource, NY*: Smithsonian American Art Museum, Washington, DC, 27. *Northwind Picture Archives*: 29, 35, 43 (top), 53 (middle). *Scotts Bluff National Park*: 33. *Bridgeman Art Library*: Chicago Historial Society, 43 (bottom). *The Image Works*: Mark Godfrey, 44. *Getty Images*: Hulton Archive, 52 (top). *Index Stock*: Grant Heilman Photography, 55; Tom Dietrich, 66. *Envison Stock Photography*: Steven Needham, 68, 73 (top); George Mattei, 72 (bottom).

Book design by Anahid Hamparian

Printed in Malaysia

1   3   5   6   4   2

Contents

A Quick Look at Nebraska

Nickname: The Cornhusker State

Population: 1,747,214 (2004 estimate)

Statehood: March 1, 1867

Flower: Goldenrod

Several species—or types—of the state flower thrive in the soils of Nebraska. In the 1800s, Ida Brockman, daughter of a state lawmaker, wrote an article in support of the flower, saying "It is native, and only a true native should be our representative. It has a long season, and nothing could better represent the hardy endurance of Nebraska's pioneers." The goldenrod was declared the state flower in 1895.

Tree: Eastern Cottonwood

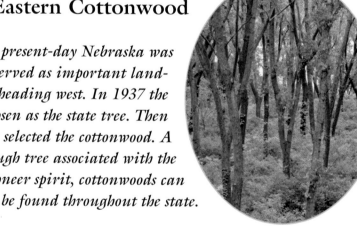

Hundreds of years ago, when present-day Nebraska was still a territory, cottonwoods served as important landmarks for pioneers heading west. In 1937 the American elm was first chosen as the state tree. Then in 1972 the state legislature selected the cottonwood. A tough tree associated with the pioneer spirit, cottonwoods can be found throughout the state.

Bird: Western Meadowlark

The western meadowlark was officially adopted as the state bird in 1929. This symbol of the plains is known for the bubbling tones of its gentle song. Well adapted to prairie life, these birds nest on the ground in secluded areas in fields and meadows.

Mammal: White-tailed Deer

In 1981 the state legislature named the white-tailed deer the official state mammal. These plant-eaters are a common sight in the forests, meadows, and cornfields of the state. Males have antlers that they shed in the winter and then grow again in early spring. Females typically give birth to one or two fawns. The babies usually have white spots on their fur. The spots often disappear by the time the fawn is one year old.

Fish: Channel Catfish

This popular sport fish can weigh up to 60 pounds. It gets its cat-related name from the eight "whiskers" growing from its chin. These are actually barbels covered in taste buds. You can identify channel catfish by their narrow heads, forked tails, and rounded fins. Channel catfish are commonly found along the gravelly bottoms of streams and lakes. The channel catfish was named the state fish in 1997.

Fossil: Mammoth

Mammoths roamed the lands of present-day North America millions of years ago. The bones of the largest mammoth ever found were uncovered in Lincoln County in west-central Nebraska. When the time came to choose a state fossil, lawmakers felt the mammoth was the best choice. These prehistoric beasts are extinct, but visitors can catch a glimpse of Archie, the life-size bronze replica of a mammoth, standing guard outside the University of Nebraska State Museum.

1 The Cornhusker State

The landscape of Nebraska is as varied as its people. Stately towers of rock jut into the sky, like lookouts stationed above the rolling prairie below. Shallow rivers and streams drift across the state, many bordered by clifflike formations called buttes. Much of the land surface of the state is marked by gentle, sloping plains. The land gently increases in elevation as the state spreads to the west.

One word that could be used to describe Nebraska is *timeless.* Rambling across the state, it is possible to imagine the Native Americans that once hunted the plains or the long trains of prairie schooners, or covered wagons, that slowly inched their way west. The state's forested bluffs and tallgrass prairies have changed little from the time these first settlers entered the state.

Nebraska's Borders
North: South Dakota
East: Iowa and Missouri
South: Kansas
South and West: Colorado
West: Wyoming

Still, Nebraska has seen many changes. What military explorer Stephen Long called the "Great Desert" in 1820 is now dotted with human-made lakes and reservoirs. Suburbs and cities have come to a land where once the only skyscraper was the spire of Chimney Rock piercing the horizon in the western part of the state.

But it is this balance of close-knit communities and wide-open spaces, of the timeless landscape and the modern world that many Nebraskans find so appealing. From rushing rivers to the vast prairie to the wild moonscapes that mark parts of the panhandle, Nebraska has it all. As one resident of Chadron noted, "It's America's best-kept secret."

Eastern Nebraska

The Missouri River forms the entire eastern border of the state. It runs along part of the state's northern border as well. Nebraska is the only state located entirely within that great river's basin. "Big

The Missouri River winds its way across the state. Near Decatur, it reaches an average depth of around 20 feet.

Muddy," as the Missouri River is often called, is a lifeline to the region, a major waterway known for its rich history and varied beauty. Lined in places by chalkstone bluffs, the river's many islands and sandbars serve as reminders of the challenges early riverboat captains faced as they chugged along the gentle waters.

Gentle valleys and rolling hills mark this part of the state. The crests, or tops, of these often steep hills are generally rounded, worn down by years of erosion. The hills are partly made up of what is called glacial till. Millions of years ago, massive glaciers had spread into the heart of the North American continent. As the climate changed and the last Ice Age ended, these giant sheets of ice slowly retreated north. Along the way, they tilled, or churned and ground up, the soil beneath. What was left behind was a deep and rich layer known as till. Later, dirt and dust carried by the wind (and known as loess) added another layer to the Nebraskan landscape. Loess makes up the eastern third of the state, including the region south of the Platte River. Over the years, rivers and streams cut their way through the region, giving the land the look it bears today.

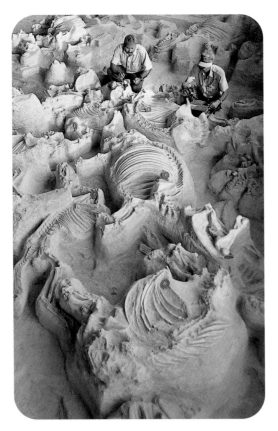

Ancient bones can be found at the Ashfall Fossil Beds State Historical Park in northeastern Nebraska. The remains of birds, turtles, horses, camels, rhinos, wild dogs, deer, and even the seeds of trees and grasses have been found there.

Today this part of the state is marked by farms and communities. More than four-fifths of Nebraska's population live in this part of the state. Omaha, the state's largest city, is found there as well. With its blend of big-city life and laid-back small-town atmosphere, many find it an ideal setting. Some even call it "the perfect place to live." Others prefer Lincoln, the state's capital, located less than an hour to the southwest of Omaha. This university town also draws students from across the country and around the world.

The Great Plains

For many, when they think of Nebraska, the first image that comes to mind is the Great Plains. Stretching westward, nearly three-quarters of the state are covered by the prairies and grasslands that make up the Great Plains and mark the

Grass, grass everywhere. Nebraska is known for its practically treeless plains. Early settlers used sod—blocks of earth and grass roots—to build their simple shelters in the early days of the territory.

American heartland. This plains region stretches beyond the state line into neighboring Wyoming and Colorado.

Included in this area are the High Plains, reaching into north-central and western Nebraska. With its towering rock formations, steep buttes, eroded hills, and deep canyons, this part of Nebraska offers some of the state's most unusual sights. The western stretch of the High Plains contains its own share of rugged beauty. Blanketed in evergreen trees, Wildcat and Pine ridges offer some of the state's most memorable scenery.

From its southeastern corner to the High Plains of the west, the state slowly gains elevation. Near the border with Wyoming, the land is more than a mile above sea level. So it is not surprising that the area is home to the state's highest point. Found in Kimball County in the southwestern tip of the Panhandle, this part of Nebraska reaches 5,426 feet.

Loess covers the central and southern plains. The landscape here is not as flat as many believe. Rolling hills break up the flatter, wide-open spaces. In south-central Nebraska is a heavily farmed part of the prairie

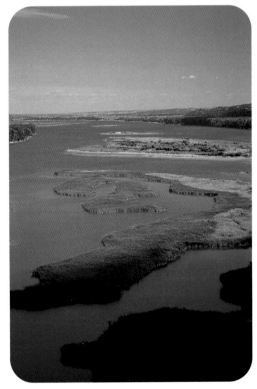

A region of the state known as the Nebraska Everglades reveals yet another unique natural feature found in the Cornhusker State. The area borders two major rivers and several lakes. Marshy patches and stretches of open water show the curious traveler that Nebraska is much more than a flat, grassy plain.

called the Loess Plains. Flat and regular, it covers roughly 7,000 square miles.

In general the plains receive little rain, which often poses a threat to farmers. Nebraska's farmers have led the way in developing systems of irrigation that help them make a living out of the land. Nebraskans are currently the largest producers and users of center-pivot irrigation. This system allows more water to be spread over a larger area. It helps thirsty plants get the water they need, without wasting what in Nebraska is a valuable resource.

The Sandhills

Covering most of north-central Nebraska is one of the state's most unique regions. The Sandhills are the largest stable sand-dune groupings in the Northern Hemisphere. Still considered a part of the Great Plains, the Nebraska Sandhills were probably blown in from the west, first forming nearly 10,000 years ago. When Zebulon Pike passed through the region, he wrote "this area may in time become as famous as the deserts of Africa." While his prediction did not come entirely true, it is still a unique region nonetheless.

The Sandhills cover about 20,000 square miles, or one-fourth of the state. The surrounding region is dotted with various marshes and lakes. This is Nebraska's cattle country. The area's wealth of water—in the form of streams and wells—and rich supply of grass have helped ranching to thrive.

> *. . . a great desert of moving sand, where there is neither soil, timber, or rock*
>
> —Scotsman James MacKay on a visit to the Sandhills in 1795

The Sandhills are a fascinating part of the state. The region—which is the largest stable sand-dune grouping in the Northern Hemisphere—resembles a desert covered in grass or a sea of gently bobbing dunes.

The wind has played a major role in shaping this part of the state. It has shifted and piled billions of grains of sand to form the ridges and hills that seem to fold back onto themselves. Some find the Sandhills the wrong name for the region, as there is little sand in sight. Instead, the thin layer of soil sports a mixed carpet of tall and shortgrass prairie. The grasses filled in and helped to bind the surface of the Sandhills, holding them in place.

But once a rip or crack is opened in this fragile surface, the contents underneath begin to spill out. The sand is lifted and carried by the wind, and soon a deep dent is left in the earth. These are called blowouts. They are usually patched by placing layers of old tires or even entire old cars in the holes. This makes the area around the blowout more stable and encourages the grass to return, repairing and resealing the holes.

The Panhandle

The Panhandle is home to some of the state's most striking features. Toadstool Geologic Park marks a part of the state commonly called the Badlands. The land buckles and folds, twisting and turning into a vast array of unusual shapes. The "toadstools," or mushrooms, found in the park are actually slabs of sandstone perched on top of "stems" made of brule clay. These strange formations were sculpted by wind and water over thousands of years. The soft clay bases eroded more quickly than their sandstone caps and thus suggested the shape of giant mushrooms. Eventually the toadstools collapse under the weight of the sandstone. But new ones continue to form to replace them.

The state's name comes from the Oto Indian word *Nebrathka,* meaning "flat water," used to describe the Platte River.

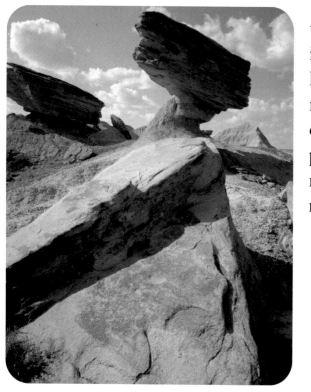

With its wealth of fossils, the park also offers a window into what life was like in the heart of the continent 38 to 24 million years ago. Still visible on some of the rocks are the preserved tracks of ancient animals that passed through the region.

Years of wind and water have shaped the sandstone slabs found in Toadstool Geologic Park in the state's Panhandle. Visitors are encouraged to ramble through the park's bizarre shapes, but bring plenty of water and watch out for the rattlesnakes!

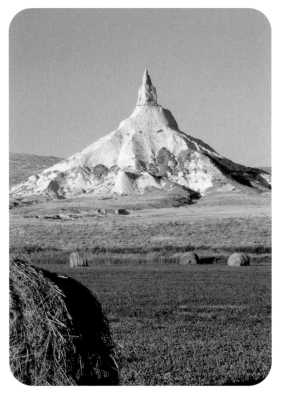

Settlers heading west by covered wagon and on foot could see Chimney Rock getting slowly larger and closer as they approached it from the east.

Hugging the southern part of the Panhandle are two impressive landmarks. Chimney Rock stands like a beacon above the plains and can be seen for miles around.

It stretches 500 feet above the Platte River and is made of brule clay, volcanic ash, and Arickaree sandstone. Scotts Bluff is another unexpected sight, rising out of the prairie. A huge plateau, it towers 800 feet. The peak can be reached on foot or by car and offers sweeping views of the countryside for more than 100 miles in all directions. These two unique features became well known to the pioneers inching their way across the plains along the Oregon Trail. Like prairie signposts, they marked the end of roughly one-third of the journey from Kansas City to the West Coast.

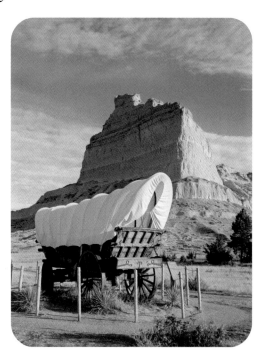

For weary pioneer travelers, Scotts Bluff offered only a hint of the towering mountain ranges they would soon face in the West.

Also found in the Panhandle is one of the nation's richest fossil beds. Preserved so it can be studied and enjoyed by countless generations, Agate Fossil Beds National Monument allows visitors to peer deep into the ancient past. The park contains the fossil evidence of the wealth of mammals that lived in the region during the Miocene period, 20 million years ago. Clearly Nebraska was a much different place then. Small, two-horned rhinoceroses, ten-foot-long predator pigs, and a mammal—described as a combination of a horse, giraffe, tapir, and a bear—roamed the grasslands.

Among the most unusual finds at the site are the preserved burrows of a land beaver called *Paleocastor.* Like today's prairie dogs, these large rodents lived together in dens tucked deep beneath the surface of the plains. They created spiral-shaped burrows that spun round and round, dug deep into ancient riverbanks. Early discoverers of the twisting chutes were baffled, calling them *Deamonelix,* or the "devil's corkscrews." Scientists believe the unique structures may have been used to confuse and stop curious predators that entered the burrows in search of a meal.

If all of Nebraska's underground water reserves were somehow brought to the surface, they would cover the state in 38 feet of liquid.

Climate

In a state where farming is so important, climate and weather can be major concerns. *Drought* is the word that makes many people cringe across the Cornhusker State. While southeastern Nebraska can receive up to 30 inches of rain and other precipitation, the Panhandle is much drier with averages totaling 17 inches. In recent years, droughts affecting the state have ranged from mild to severe. But there is little that can be done to control the weather. Still, to show how important the subject is, the state has set up two agencies to focus on weather issues and concerns. The Climate Assessment and Response Committee and the Nebraska State Climate Office study weather trends and provide forecasts and advice in dealing with the often harsh conditions.

Nebraska generally has a mild climate. Warm summers, cold but not-too-snowy winters, lots of sunshine, and average humidity are the rule. Nonetheless, state residents have learned to adjust to the occasional seasonal extremes. Nebraskans also know that the expected can turn into the unexpected in a flash—of lightning, that is. Early evening thunderstorms are a common event in the summertime, especially in the eastern and central portions of the state. The sky blackens and thick masses of clouds churn in the sky. With their state located squarely in the line of what is called America's Tornado Alley, Nebraskans know that, at certain times, when storms come blowing, it is best to run for cover. Tornados have ripped across the state, causing countless damage and threatening lives.

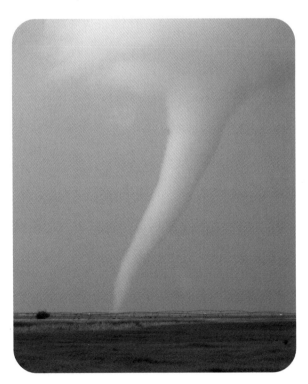

A tornado can spell disaster to a Nebraska farmer. This one spins and snakes its way across the fields outside Stuart.

Storm chasers, people who follow and study tornados and other dramatic weather events, find Nebraska a prime hunting ground. A team of these curious thrill-seekers travels throughout the Midwest in the spring and summer. They drive special storm-chasing vehicles, equipped with Doppler radar and other devices that allow them to collect data and to track and study storms. Another storm-chasing tool is the IMAX tornado-intercept vehicles. They allow movie makers to film tornados from as close as possible. Currently in development is a cruiser that may allow film crews to drive inside these swirling and dangerous storm systems.

Wild Life

Although forests cover only 2 percent of the state, Nebraska still has its share of trees. Oaks, elms, boxelders, basswood, ash, and hackberry are just a few of the trees that can be seen wafting in the prairie winds. One of the state's major wooded areas can be found along the Niobrara River valley. It took root in the moist, rich soil and spread from the east, almost halfway across the state. To the northwest, the rugged Pine Ridge region is another trove of tree life. As its name implies, it is an area known for its impressive stands of pine.

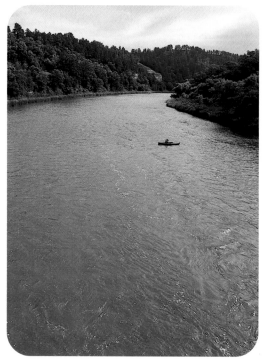

The tree-lined Niobrara River swells and surges as it makes its way across northern Nebraska.

Perhaps the state's most impressive forest, though, is the product of its hardworking residents. The first United States Forest Service nursery in the country is the Nebraska State Forest. Located near Halsey, it is the world's largest woodland planted entirely by hand. The forest was originally created to draw potential settlers to the otherwise barren region. Few settlers came, but the trees helped to curb erosion and to prevent the dusty topsoil from being carried away by the wind.

The most common form of plant life in the Cornhusker State is the wealth of native prairie grasses that the state is known for. These varied species house, hide, and feed an equally impressive array of animal life. Mule deer, white-tailed deer, pronghorn antelope, bison, elk, and bighorn sheep are just a few of the four-footed creatures that make the state their home. Coyotes and bobcats pad across the prairie in search of food, while along the state's rivers and streams, beavers, muskrats, and mink thrive. Raccoons are drawn to the water as well to try their hand at fishing. Trout, perch, bass, catfish, carp, pike, and crappies abound beneath the surface of the state's many waterways.

With so many crane-watchers descending on the state each year, it is clear that Nebraska is a bird-watcher's paradise. Dedicated birders also enjoy the mating calls and elaborate dances of the prairie chicken and sharp-tailed grouse. Pheasants, quail, ducks, snow geese, turkey vultures, whippoorwills, great horned owls, and wild turkeys are among the species found in the state. Golden eagles and prairie falcons soar over the grasslands, their sharp eyes searching for rodents and prairie dogs below. Cliff swallows also make an annual appearance in Nebraska. They fly more than 3,000 miles from Argentina to nest in the state's lake-filled southwestern corner.

Plants & Animals

Prairie Rattlesnake

The prairie rattler is one of only four species of poisonous snakes living in Nebraska. They are usually found in the western two-thirds of the state on the plains and grasslands. Mostly active in the daytime, these reptiles live off a diet of rabbits, prairie dogs, kangaroo rats, mice, and lizards.

Coyote

Cautious and highly intelligent, the coyote is a relative of the wolf. Coyotes are mostly active at night, when their sharp barks and howling can be heard drifting across the plains. Coyotes eat birds, insects, dead animals, rodents, and rabbits. They have also been known to stray onto farmers' and ranchers' lands to prey on small livestock.

Pronghorn Antelope

Most of Nebraska's pronghorns are found in the western Panhandle, but smaller populations are located in the Sandhills and central areas of the state as well. Drought and the spread of farms have affected the antelope population. But officials are confident that these nimble mammals—known for their great speed and powerful eyesight—will continue to thrive in the Cornhusker State.

Prairie Chicken

These peculiar birds were once an important food source for Native Americans and settlers living on the plains. Hunters shipped wagonfuls of prairie chickens to the East. Through the years, the prairie chickens' range and numbers have greatly shrunk. Today a small but growing population makes its home mostly in the central and southeastern portions of Nebraska.

Sandhill Crane

These powerful fliers mate for life and can live up to twenty-five years. Sandhill cranes have been stopping over in Nebraska, during their annual migrations, for thousands of years. More than half a million birds gather each spring along the Platte River before heading to their summer breeding grounds.

Little Bluestem

Also known as bunch grass or beard grass, little bluestem is found across the Great Plains. It commonly grows in clumps of up to three hundred reddish purple stems, which turn a golden color as the plant ages. Little bluestem can reach only a few inches in height in poor soil or up to 3 feet in the moister parts of the plains.

Endangered

With so many natural treasures, Nebraskans have made strong efforts to protect the land and the life it supports. The state currently has thirteen species of plants and animals on its list of endangered species. Programs and agencies have been created to make sure the list does not grow. Black-footed ferrets, wolves, and grizzly bears once roamed the plains freely. But with the arrival of settlers from the East, some animal populations decreased, and are now a rare sight in the Cornhusker State. The swift fox, the prairie chicken, and many others species were once found in large numbers. Today that is not the case.

Blowout penstemon is a flowering plant found mainly in the Sandhills. Now endangered, efforts have been made by scientists to try to grow more of these blue-flowered plants.

Sometimes the best conservation plans help to protect animals long before a species is threatened or endangered. Every year, more and more visitors flock to the 80-mile stretch of the Platte River to witness the annual migration of more than half a million cranes. The birds have become a popular attraction each March, as they stop along the river to rest and feed before flying on to their breeding grounds in Canada, Alaska, and parts of Siberia. About 80 percent of the world's population of sandhill cranes passes through the region every year.

The increased tourism has helped the economy of this part of the state. Still, many local residents, biologists, and officials have realized that this success cannot come at a cost to the birds. While the birds have been traveling to the area for thousands of years, if their habitat is harmed or threatened, or if they feel the pressure of too many people, they may choose another location to stop over on their annual migration.

Two recent million-dollar projects have taken great strides in ensuring the safety and future of Nebraska's beloved seasonal visitors. The Crane Meadows Nature Center, located outside Wood River, offers three blinds—or enclosed shelters—to morning and evening visitors. To the west, the National Audubon Society's Lillian Annette Rowe Bird Sanctuary in Gibbon offers bird-watchers four blinds. The famed nature magazine *National Geographic* has also set up a live, online video feed of the cranes for those who cannot make it to the site in person.

The birds have become popular tourist attractions, each year drawing more and more people from across Nebraska and around the world. With these two new centers, humans and cranes now have the ideal settings in which to coexist. Wildlife centers such as these show that Nebraskans wish to provide a safe, welcoming place for all its visitors, whether they be animal or human.

A majestic symbol of the state, sandhill cranes gather in the shallow waters of the Platte River near Kearney.

2 From the Beginning

Humans first entered the central plains around 12,000 years ago, near the end of the last Ice Age. They were mostly hunters, following roving herds of big game. These people, often called the Paleo-Indians, were the ancestors of the Native Americans who would eventually spread across the state. Over thousands of years, these ancient peoples lived on the grasslands that would become the future state of Nebraska. Slowly, weather and climate patterns shifted and became more stable. This, as well as the extinction of several prehistoric species such as the mammoth, encouraged the creation of more permanent settlements. The Paleo-Indians continued hunting and gathering, but eventually started to farm plots of land in and near their villages.

By 2,000 years ago, more complex communities dotted the plains. These early residents made helpful, everyday items out of pottery. They also fished in Nebraska's many rivers and grew to rely more heavily on agriculture. Nebraska was a harsh region to conquer. Periods of drought forced some groups to

Immigrants and pioneers came at different times, slowly taming the plains that would form the future state of Nebraska. This family settled in the Loup Valley in 1886.

pack up and search for a better life elsewhere. During times of prosperity, many sought out the future state. The region quickly became a crossroads of Native American life. Even in its earliest days, the state was a lively and diverse mixture of various native languages and culture groups.

Native Nebraska

The region that was to become Nebraska was settled by several mighty Native American nations. They came to dominate the central plains well into the 1830s. The Pawnee, and their northern relatives the Arikaras, left perhaps the deepest mark on the region. They first arrived in Nebraska from the south and were well established there by the mid-1500s. They built earthen lodges made of

In the 1860s, frontier artist William Henry Jackson traveled across the Nebraska territory painting scenes, such as this Pawnee village, along the way. Once one of the region's major Native groups, by 1875, the territory's remaining five hundred Pawnee had been forced to relocate to Oklahoma.

stacked poles covered with brush and packed with mud. These striking structures were a common sight, grouped into villages huddled along the banks of the Platte, Loup, and Republican rivers, to name a few.

Other groups left their mark as well. The Cheyenne, Arapaho, and Lakota (Teton Sioux) pushed west after originally settling in the forests north and east of the Missouri River. The Omaha, Ponca, and Oto were also transplants to the area. They entered the eastern portion of the state in the 1700s and lived in the Missouri River basin as well. By the start of the 1800s, about 40,000 Native Americans called Nebraska home.

George Catlin produced this image of Big Elk, an Omaha warrior in 1832. The Omaha had originally come from the East, eventually settling in the regions that now include Nebraska and South Dakota.

The arrival of European explorers and settlers changed the Native Americans' lives forever. The introduction of the horse meant they could travel and hunt more effectively. But diseases such as measles and smallpox swept through entire villages, leaving very few standing. Eventually the valuable land the Native Americans held was too tempting to arriving settlers, and the Native people were slowly driven from the land. Treaties were made. But not all the land deals between the United States government and the various Native nations had been made final by the 1850s when the area became a territory that was suddenly opened for settlement.

The First Europeans

The first European to make an appearance in the region was Francisco Vasquez de Coronado. He and a crew of men trekked across the American Southwest in 1541, making it all the way to Kansas. The explorer claimed the entire region for Spain.

Coming from a different direction, French explorer Rene Robert Cavalier, sieur de la Salle, sailed down the Mississippi River in 1682. Though he never set foot in the future state, he claimed all the land drained by the river for King Louis XIV, the ruler of France. This was just the first step in opening the region to curious Europeans seeking their fortune along the American frontier. During the 1690s and early 1700s, trappers and traders crisscrossed the region. By 1714 the French explorer Étienne Veniard de Bourgmont had followed the course of the Missouri River all the way to the mouth of the Platte.

With competing claims on the continent, Spain and France became rivals for power and control of the New World. The Nebraska region became one source of the conflict. Feeling the French had overstepped their bounds, Spaniard Pedro de Villasur led a group of forty-five men into the area in 1720 with the hopes of expelling, or removing, the French. But before it could do so, the group was attacked by Pawnee warriors near the Platte River. In the battle that followed, most of the Spaniards were killed. So the French remained, holding tightly to their foothold in Nebraska.

> *Well-beaten paths, broad prairies, hills, many trees loaded with hazelnuts along the brooks and the little valleys. Deer were there in herds.*
>
> —an entry from Bourgmont's journal, July 4, 1724

In simple canoes and on foot, the region's first explorers slowly mapped the lands that would form the future state.

In 1739 the French explorers Paul and Pierre Mallet, joined by six others, left Illinois in the hope of reaching present-day Santa Fe, New Mexico. Along the way they crossed almost the entire length of Nebraska. They also named the Platte River. Slowly the territory that was to become Nebraska was being mapped and tamed. But events in Europe would cause the region to change hands several times. In 1763, after a costly war in Europe, France gave up all of its land claims west of the Mississippi River to Spain. Like before, French fur traders were still working in the Spanish-controlled region.

For the time being, they were wise in staying, because in 1800, French leader Napoléon Bonaparte forced the Spanish to return the land. French control was to be short-lived, though. Three years later, in need of funds, Bonaparte sold the large territory, referred to as the Louisiana Purchase, to the United States government.

The Americans Arrive

With so much newly acquired land, the Americans were eager to explore their recent purchase. Meriwether Lewis and William Clark and their Corps of Discovery spent three months in the state, starting in 1804. They traveled up the Missouri River and explored what are now the eastern and northern borders of Nebraska. Then, in 1806, Zebulon Pike, on a similar mission, entered and explored south-central Nebraska.

It was not long before trading posts sprang up in the Missouri River valley. The Spanish-American trader Manuel Lisa established a string of them from 1807 to 1820. Fort Lisa, one of the posts, was located 10 miles from present-day Omaha. The economy of this once-remote region was developing slowly. Trappers and traders, looking to cash in on the wealth of furs they could find to the west, continued to pass through the region. In 1812 fur agent Robert Stuart left Astoria in the Oregon Territory and headed for New York City. Entering Nebraska in 1813, Stuart and his seven companions followed the course of the North Platte River to the point where it joins the South Platte. They then continued along, following the river until it met up with the Missouri River. It would prove to be an ideal path to follow, and the future course of the Oregon Trail, which brought countless pioneers deep into the American West.

In 1819 the United States Army arrived to build Nebraska's first military post, Fort Atkinson. It was established near the present-day town of Fort Calhoun located in Washington County. Intended to protect the American frontier, the site became, along with the village of Bellevue, one of the largest communities in Nebraska at the time. With more than 1,000 residents, Fort Atkinson set up the state's first school, library, and grist mill.

The fort was eventually abandoned in 1827.

A year after the army arrived, Major Stephen Long and a group of twenty men followed the South Platte to its source near present-day Denver, Colorado. Major Long's now-famous reports talk of a barren and harsh land, unfit for humans. He held little hope that the region would one day prosper. On the simple map that a member of Long's expedition drew, the major had this area, which includes present-day Nebraska, labeled the "Great Desert."

Luckily, Major Long's impressions were wrong. Nebraska would become a thriving territory in no time. Missionaries

. . . a barren and uncongenial [unpleasant] district
—Major Stephen Long's first impression of Nebraska

This log cabin at Fort Atkinson State Historical Park bears witness to the state's earliest days, when non-Native communities were first forming.

appeared, including the famed Catholic priest Father de Smet, who was eager to work with the Nebraska and Pawnee Native Americans. Fur traders continued to come and go, spreading through the region. They especially flocked to the Platte River route, which quickly grew in popularity. In little more than two decades, Long's great desert would become flooded with thousands of pioneers, eager for a better life in the American West.

The Territory Grows

As more and more American settlers searched for their fortunes in the West, Nebraska became an important center of activity. Both the Oregon Trail and the Mormon Trail wound their way through the region. Pony Express riders followed the well-worn routes that traveled through the Platte River valley. Before the arrival of the railroad, steamboats were important to the trade and transportation of the region.

With so much increased traffic, Fort Kearny was built to offer added protection for the hopeful pioneers headed west. Though white settlers flooded the area, most were only passing through. Nebraska was still considered Native American territory, and non-Native families were not allowed to settle there.

By the 1840s, Nebraska was on the road to statehood. Secretary of War William Wilkins, in a report from 1844, stated "The Platte or Nebraska River being the central stream would very properly furnish a name to the territory." It was in that year that the first attempt was made to make the area a territory. But the measure failed to pass. Another bill, known as the Nebraska-Kansas Act, was eventually approved in 1854 after much debate and disagreement. It officially created the Kansas

Fort Kearny was the first military post set up to protect the travelers heading west. It was a good stopping point where pioneers could buy food and other much-needed supplies.

and Nebraska territories and allowed the citizens to decide whether or not slavery would be allowed. Most Nebraskans were against the practice.

The two new regions were created in the hope of increasing settlement west of the Missouri River. Originally the Nebraska Territory was much larger than the state is today. In addition to Nebraska, it included parts of the present-day states of Montana, Wyoming, Colorado, and North and South Dakota. By 1863 the territory had been divided further, leaving Nebraska close to the size and shape it is today.

By this time, the nation was deeply divided over the issue of slavery. Those opposed to the practice were worried that the new territories would allow slavery. Those in favor of slavery believed there was no question whether or not it would be allowed in the newly created lands. Both sides clashed and minor conflicts were fought in the region long before the first cannons of the Civil War were fired. (The slavery issue was one of the main reasons for the Civil War.) Slaves were first bought and sold in Nebraska in the 1850s in Nebraska City.

Slavery was not the only issue dividing the newly created territory. Residents and officials disagreed over how the territory would be settled, the creation of new laws, the coming of the railroad, and, most notably, the location of the territorial capital. In addition, there were often regional rivalries between those living north of the Platte River and those who had settled to the south. Many issues remained to be worked out, and the territory was denied statehood when it first attempted to join the Union. Still, the area prospered. From 1854 to 1860, Nebraska's population grew from 2,732 to 28,841.

The Civil War and Beyond

During the Civil War, the residents of the Nebraska Territory generally supported the Union, or Northern, forces. Volunteers helped form the First Nebraska Infantry under the command of Colonel John M. Thayer. Although disagreement still ran deep among many Nebraskans, the battles never entered the territory and affected the region less than the states located farther to the east.

The passage of the Homestead Act in 1862 increased the territory's population all the more. It granted settlers 160 acres of free western land if they agreed to live and work on it. More hopeful pioneers came to try their hand at working the

Nebraska countryside.

The major event of the decade was the coming of the Union Pacific Railroad. A line extending westward from Omaha was started in 1865. It reached the western border of the territory two years later. Throughout the 1870s and 1880s, the railroads were big business in the state and did much to change the life of the region. To spur the growth and number of railroad lines and to further connect the growing country, the United States government offered certain companies portions of the territory in the form of land grants.

By the end of the 1800s, many Nebraska communities were connected to the world beyond through the miles and miles of rails.

To raise funds in order to build the rail lines, the companies in turn sold large tracts of the land to interested settlers. They often created elaborate ad campaigns to lure new arrivals not only from the East Coast but from Europe as well. The ad campaigns worked. Along with a flood of former Civil War soldiers who also arrived in the region in search of land, the population of Nebraska ballooned to almost 123,000 by 1870. By the mid-1880s the Burlington Railroad lines also crossed the state. Once-remote areas now found themselves in greater contact with the world beyond.

Making a Bandbox

In the 1800s people traveling to Nebraska—and to other parts of the country—used bandboxes to carry small objects like gloves and jewelry. The first bandboxes were made by shirt manufacturers to ship men's stiff shirt collars (these collars were called bands).

People found the boxes useful for storage as well as travel. They lined the inside of the box with newspaper and decorated the outside with colorful wallpaper. Following these instructions you can make your own bandbox.

What You Need

Several sheets of newspaper
An empty round oatmeal container-or a similar
    container
Tape measure and ruler
Pencil
Heavy gift wrapping paper or wallpaper (a square about 36 inches
    by 36 inches)
Scissors
Craft glue
Small part of a sponge
Ribbon (about 20 inches long; 3/4 to
    1 inch wide)

Spread the newspaper on your work surface and place the wallpaper or wrapping paper on it, design-side down. Use the tape measure to measure the distance around the container and the height. Add one inch to the distance. Measure a piece of the

wallpaper using the distance (plus the one inch) as the length of the wallpaper piece. The height of the container will serve as the width of the wallpaper piece. Cut the piece.

Have an adult help you with these next steps. Spread glue on the back of the wallpaper piece. Use a damp sponge to spread the glue thinly and evenly. Center the container on the glue-covered paper. Make sure that the top and bottom edges of the paper are lined up with the top and bottom edges of the container. Carefully roll the container across the paper, making sure the paper sticks to the container. Smooth out any air bubbles that form between the paper and the container.

To decorate the lid, lay some of the remaining wallpaper against your work surface-design-side down. Place the lid on the paper and trace around the circle with a pencil. Cut out the circle, spread glue, and stick the paper to the lid. Use small strips of the wallpaper to cover the edges of the lid. Glue the middle of the ribbon to the bottom of your container. (The ribbon should be about 2 1/2 times the height of the container.) Run the ribbon up the sides of the bandbox, using drops of glue to keep it in place. The ribbon should stretch beyond the ends of the container. When the lid is on the bandbox, you can bring the ribbons over the top and tie a bow to keep the box closed. When the glue is dry your bandbox is ready. You can use it to store things or you can use it when giving gifts.

Statehood

Nebraska was finally admitted to the Union on March 1, 1867, but again, not without conflict. The president serving at the time, Andrew Johnson, was a Democrat and did not want the mostly Republican territory to be offered statehood. He vetoed, or rejected, the act of Congress making Nebraska a state. Congress was able to override Johnson's veto. But lawmakers set down their own terms the territory had to meet before it was allowed into the Union. The Nebraska legislature had to remove a phrase from its proposed state constitution that gave only free white men the right to vote.

The early years of statehood were rough on Nebraska. It was a pattern that had become all too familiar. As was the case with some of Nebraska's early Native cultures, the harsh conditions of life on the prairie proved too challenging for some residents. When swarms of grasshoppers descended on the state and destroyed countless acres of crops, many farm families packed up and headed back east. The state's economy did not surge in the 1870s, and recovery was slow in coming.

Eaten out by grasshoppers. Going back East to live with wife's folks.
—sign on a wagon seen leaving Nebraska, 1876

By the 1880s, though, the tide had turned. Another large wave of settlers came to the state. New residents, eager for their own homesteads, arrived on the plains. Land prices increased steadily throughout the decade. Once again, however, with the arrival of the 1890s, the state faced hard times. Drought settled on the land, and real estate prices dropped. Many farmers found themselves bankrupt.

With few trees to supply building materials, resourceful residents built their homes from thick blocks of sod. This family settled in Custer County in the 1880s.

Many people called out for change. Farmers felt banks and railroads were concerned only with their own profits. Families and other small operations could not afford the high prices the railroads charged to ship crops and other farm products. Hundreds of Nebraska farmers turned to a new organization called the Farmers' Alliance. It worked to reduce shipping costs and curb the power of large companies.

The Twentieth Century

Nebraskans had long been inventive when it came to coaxing a living out of the often harsh landscape. New techniques had been developed for irrigating, or watering, the dry soil. To help the state along, Congress passed the Reclamation Act in 1902.

It created funds to encourage and improve irrigation systems, such as the North Platte Project, which helped irrigate 165,000 acres of Nebraskan land. In the Panhandle, where farming could be especially challenging, new crops were able to thrive. Sugar beets, alfalfa, and winter wheat are major crops still grown in the state today.

In central and western Nebraska, farmers and ranchers had often clashed. Ranchers often resented the presence of farmers, who claimed land the ranchers felt could be better used for raising cattle. With Congress's passage of the Kinkaid Act, though, the farmers scored a victory. It allowed farmers to increase their holdings up to 640 acres and thus have a greater chance to make a success of their ventures. As a result of the act, the Sandhills saw greater development. Though many found the area too harsh to farm successfully, their efforts still helped build the area's economy. While the Sandhills did not lend themselves easily to farming, it was ideal cattle country. Ranchers bought the failed farms and expanded their holdings in the area. They fattened their herds on the acres of grassland.

World War I brought great change to the nation, especially Nebraska. While many brave Cornhuskers were off fighting in Europe, the state's economy boomed. There was a great demand for the wealth of farm products Nebraska produced. With the end of the war in 1919, though, the economy slumped once again. Then in 1929 came the ultimate blow. The Great Depression gripped the country and eventually the world. Jobs were scarce, people were out of work and there was little relief in sight. The price of farm products dipped even further. Yet another drought made matters only worse. Farmers

Massive erosion only added to the tragedies brought by the Great Depression. A lone farmer looks on in disbelief at his dry, eroding land in Richardson County.

lost their land. Relief in the form of long-term, low-interest loans provided some help, but the lean years left few Nebraskans untouched.

But most Nebraskans were not without hope. The coming of World War II brought a much-needed boost to the state's economy. Farm products were again in high demand, including cattle, oats, wheat, potatoes, and corn. The state's growing number of factories turned out war supplies. More than 128,000 Nebraskans joined the war effort, many of them fighting on the battlefields of Europe and Asia.

In the last half of the twentieth century, the state's economy changed rapidly. Still a major agricultural state, the state's farms have become larger, but fewer in number. The size of the average farm almost doubled between 1950 and the late 1990s. But there are only half the number of farms there were by the end of World War II. Advances in technology and farm machinery have meant these larger operations require fewer workers. So many Nebraskans have looked for new ways of earning a living. Some have turned to the state's cities and towns as important sources of income. During the 1960s, state leaders were able to attract new businesses, mostly in manufacturing, to the state.

As the state's economy and centers of population shifted, new challenges arose. Once a mostly rural state, Nebraskans were faced, more and more, with problems often associated with larger cities—crime, urban poverty, and racial unrest. The 1960s were a period of radical change for Nebraska's African-American residents. Civil rights demonstrations—which were held to call attention to racial inequality—took place in Omaha in 1963. Then, in 1968 and 1969, race riots in that city required the United States military and the National Guard to step in.

Meanwhile, in rural Nebraska, farmers faced challenges of their own. Farming became too expensive for some because there was little profit to show for the hours of labor required. Many families sold their farms and turned to another way of life. By 1970 more than 60 percent of the state's residents lived in Nebraska's cities and towns. The times marked a major and gradual shift away from rural life. The change made Nebraskans aware of the need to build industries and to draw new businesses to the state.

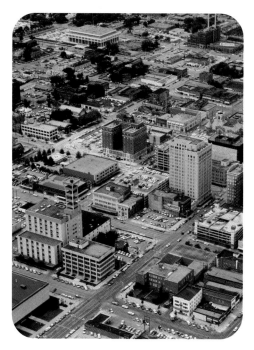

In the twenty-first century, many residents look to the future with confidence. But they also continue to honor their roots and the times of struggle and triumph that have made the state the strong, united place it is today.

As the state grew, residents began moving to the state's cities and suburban areas. This aerial view of Lincoln shows Nebraska's thriving capital.

Important Dates

1541   Spanish explorer Francisco Vasquez de Coronado leads an expedition and claims the region for Spain.

1682   French explorer Rene Robert Cavelier, Sieur de la Salle, claims the lands drained by the Mississippi River, including present-day Nebraska, for France.

1714   Étienne Veniard de Bourgmont becomes the first recorded European to enter the area now known as Nebraska.

1739   While trying to find the way to Santa Fe, Frenchmen Pierre and Paul Mallet become lost and are the first Europeans known to cross Nebraska.

1803   With the Louisiana Purchase, the United States gains possession of Nebraska.

1806   Explorer Zebulon Pike enters southern Nebraska.

1819   Fort Atkinson, the United States Army's first post in Nebraska, is built.

Zebulon Pike

1823   Traders and others found Bellevue, the state's first permanent settlement.

1840s   Thousands of travelers along the Oregon Trail pass through the Platte River valley and, eventually, past Fort Kearny.

1854   Congress passes the Kansas-Nebraska Act, allowing the territories to decide whether or not slavery will be allowed within their borders.

1862   The Homestead Act further opens the territory to settlement.

1867   Nebraska joins the Union as the thirty-seventh state.

1877   Oglala Sioux leader Crazy Horse surrenders in Nebraska.

1904   The Kincaid Act promotes settlement in the Sandhills and Panhandle.

Crazy Horse

1929   The Great Depression begins, affecting residents in Nebraska and across the country.

1968-1969 Race riots erupt in Omaha, prompting the arrival of the National Guard.

1974   Omaha's Gerald Ford becomes president of the United States.

1982   A new state law bars farmers from selling their land to corporations.

1992   The state lottery is created.

2003   Nebraska celebrates the Lewis & Clark Bicentennial Commemoration.

3 The People

Nebraskans have always been a diverse group. The state's first residents were the Native Americans who settled in the open grasslands. Other newcomers arrived as slaves, while still more came from Europe in search of a better life. Today Nebraskans trace their roots to a variety of sources. Many come from families who have lived in the state for many generations.

Through the years, people of varying backgrounds have called the state home. Starting in the 1800s, waves of immigrants began spreading across the plains. The largest ethnic groups represented in the state today trace their roots back to Germany, Ireland, England, Sweden, and the Czech and Slovak republics. But these groups are just one part of the changing face of Nebraska in the twenty-first century. Today people from across the United States and around the world are drawn to life in the Cornhusker State. Together, they form a varied and vibrant society.

A costumed re-enactor describes life on the Oregon Trail to a group of children. Nebraska's rich past has helped shape the diverse range of people who call the state home today.

Native Nebraska

Nebraska was once home to a long list of Native American groups. The Arapaho, Cheyenne, Dakota Sioux, Santee Sioux, Fox, Omaha, Oto, Pawnee, Potawatome, Ponca, and Sac are some of the major groups that made their home on the state's grasslands. These various nations once had more than 40,000 combined members. But slowly through the years, their numbers declined. By the early 1910s, less than 5,000 Native Americans remained in the state. Most had been forced to move onto reservations in nearby states.

Today, almost 15,000 Native Americans call Nebraska home. They are spread across the state in cities and towns. They also live on Nebraska's three reservations—the Santee Sioux, Winnebago, and Omaha. A small group of Sac and Fox can be found living in homes on the southeastern portion of the state.

Each year, usually in July, the Winnebago Reservation hosts a two-day gathering. Councils are held, and ancient

A powwow marks a special time for Native people to come together and celebrate the dances and rituals that make their culture unique.

traditions revived and shared. The Santee Sioux hold their annual powwow in June, while the Omaha come together each August. The events feature a variety of activities. Symbolic dances and traditional songs are performed, bringing the native past vividly to life. There is also storytelling during which native history and lore are shared and passed on. But most of all, it is a time for Nebraska's native residents to come together, visit with friends and relatives, and celebrate the bond they all share.

Czechs on the Plains

Czechs played a major role in the settling of the Cornhusker State. By 1910, 14 percent of Nebraska's foreign-born residents had come from Czechoslovakia, the largest Czech population in any state. Crop failures and a weak economy first drove many Czechs from their homeland in the 1870s and 1880s. Many would face similar problems in their new nation. Railroad advertisements—as well as glowing articles in Czech magazines and newspapers—convinced thousands to uproot their lives and try their fortune in the paradise of the American plains. Friends and relatives were a strong draw as well. Their letters and reports home spoke of the pleasures of life on the plains.

The newly arrived Czechs were mostly farmers, but merchants and laborers came, too. Many early settlements were mostly all-Czech villages. Most immigrants chose to settle together, preferring the comfort and support of their fellow countrymen to ease the transition to life in America. From the mid-1850s until World War I, Nebraska was the top destination for Czechs coming to the United States. As was the case with many plains states at the end of the 1800s, the 1870 census revealed that nearly 25 percent of Nebraskans were foreign born.

Today many Nebraskans celebrate their Czech heritage in a variety of ways. Festivals and annual events bring the culture to life. Wilber, sometimes called the Czech Capital of America, draws people from the across the Midwest and beyond. Recently, greater efforts are being made to honor and preserve the history of Czech life on the plains. The Czech Heritage Materials Preservation Project is leading the way. Working with groups at the University of Nebraska, project workers are creating an archive, or collection,

of photographs and letters that capture elements of early Czech-American life. A major part of the project involves translating cassette recordings made in the 1970s by state residents. Mostly told in the Czech language, these oral histories, as they are called, tell of life on the American plains. They are a key part of preserving Nebraska's rich Czech history. Some tell stories of coming to the United States and settling into mostly Czech communities where children often learned in Czech. Someday, project workers hope to

Round and round, these revelers perform traditional Czech dances in Wilber.

post these various materials on the Internet, making them available to all.

To keep close ties between America and the Czech Republic, the University of Nebraska-Lincoln has set up the Paul Robitschek Czech Study Program. It offers scholarships to students living in the Czech Republic. Through the program, they are given the chance to further their studies in the United States and to learn about the place many Czech people immigrated to in the 1800s and 1900s.

African Americans

African Americans have long been a part of the history of the Cornhusker State. The first census of the territory, taken in 1854, listed only four slaves. Up until the Civil War, fewer than one hundred African Americans called the state home. When the war ended—and slavery along with it—this trend changed. Slowly, people began turning west as a place to pursue their newfound freedom.

Groups of black settlers began pushing into the heart of the plains. Called Exodusters, some came to Nebraska after settling in Kansas for a while. They eventually set down roots in Lincoln, Omaha, and Nebraska City. While many worked for the railroads, others lived mostly in Custer, Dawson, and Harlan counties. An all-black community was founded at Overton in 1885. More black towns, including Brownlee

Nebraska's African-American Firsts

1870   Robert Anderson, first to homestead in the territory

1892   Matthew O. Ricketts, first to serve in the state legislature

1895   Silas Robbins, first to officially practice law in the state

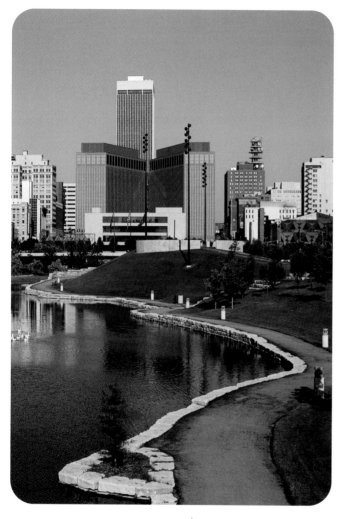

Nebraska's bustling cities—such as Omaha—have become vibrant centers for the rich cultural diversity the state has to offer.

and DeWitty, formed in the early 1900s in Cherry County. With its acres of unclaimed land, western Nebraska became a draw for many black families.

The early decades of the 1900s also marked the great migration to the North. More than 500,000 blacks left their homes in the South and headed north and west. Omaha saw the greatest change. Between 1910 and 1920, its black population doubled from around 5,000 to 10,315. Its population has grown ever since. For many African Americans living in the state, life was not always easy. Racial tensions, killings, and riots marred the lives of many.

Through it all, the state's African-American community has stayed strong. Black Nebraskans still honor the struggles of the past, as they look to the future. Today in many of Nebraska's schools the state's African-American heritage is celebrated. As countless students now learn, the history of their state cannot be told without the inclusion of the African-American experience.

New Faces

As is the case in most other states, Hispanics are Nebraska's fastest-growing group. Their numbers nearly doubled during the 1990s. The state's urban areas saw the greatest jump. Douglas County, in particular, which contains the city of Omaha, was the site of the largest rise.

But new residents have settled in all parts of Nebraska. Asian Americans have also grown in numbers. Though a smaller presence in Nebraska overall, the state's Asian community also experienced a major population jump. During the 1990s, it grew by nearly 73 percent. These figures show the broad appeal of the Cornhusker State.

People from all backgrounds are drawn to the state's peaceful communities, low crime, and strong schools. Nebraska is also an affordable place to live and raise a family. Slowly, Nebraskans are seeing their communities grow and change. While the state is still mostly white, today Nebraska sports its own vibrant blend of peoples and cultures.

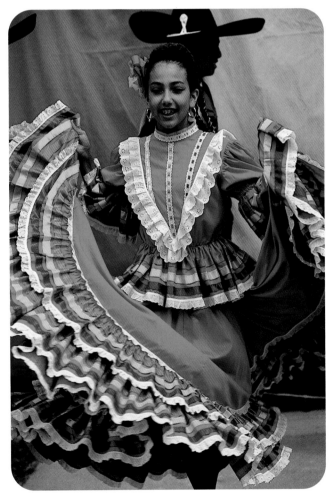

Hispanics are a fast-growing group in the Cornhusker State. With her ruffles flying, this young woman performs a traditional Mexican dance.

Famous Nebraskans

Willa Cather: Author

As a little girl, Cather and her family relocated to a barren stretch of the Nebraska plains. Though she experienced a difficult and lonely childhood, she eventually grew to love living on the prairie. Her experiences would also eventually fuel her talents as a writer. In such classics as O Pioneers!, My Antonia, *and* Song of the Lark, *she captured the joys and struggles of life in the Midwest.*

Gerald R. Ford: United States President

Born in Omaha in 1913 and raised in Michigan, in 1974, Gerald R. Ford was the first person to assume the nation's highest office after the resignation of the previous president, Richard Nixon. A lieutenant commander in the Navy during World War II, he was elected to Congress in 1948. As president, he attempted to address problems with the nation's economy. On the foreign front, he guided America's relations with the Soviet Union, the Middle East, and Southeast Asia.

Buffalo Bill Cody: Entertainer

This colorful character arrived in Nebraska Territory as an eight-year-old boy. By fourteen, he was a rider for the Pony Express. A talented hunter, Cody earned his nickname hunting buffalo on the plains. His skills as a marksman and entertainer gave rise to his famed Wild West shows, which were presented to eager audiences in America and Europe for three decades.

J. Sterling Morton:
Founder of Arbor Day

When this nature lover first arrived in Nebraska in 1854, he was shocked to find a mostly treeless stretch of prairie. A reporter and later an elected official, Morton used his power to urge people to plant trees. This led to his greatest legacy, the creation of Arbor Day, an event currently celebrated in different forms around the world. At Morton's request, state residents planted a million trees to mark the first Arbor Day on April 10, 1872.

Red Cloud: Warrior and Statesman

Also known as Makhpiya-Luta, Red Cloud was born near North Platte. He was schooled from an early age in the art of war, eventually rising to a position of power in the Lakota nation for his handling of territorial battles with the Crow, Pawnee, Ute, and Shoshone. In 1866 Red Cloud directed a successful war against the United States government, securing peace for a number of years through the Fort Laramie Treaty. He dedicated the rest of his life to resisting the advance of settlers. He also fought against American officials who unfairly seized and distributed Native-held lands. Red Cloud died in 1909.

Malcolm X: African-American Leader

In 1925, Malcolm Little was born in Omaha. In his twenties, he embraced the teachings of the Nation of Islam and changed his last name to X to reflect the loss of his true family name when his ancestors were first enslaved. Malcolm X worked to shed light on the racial abuses practiced by many whites, and was known for his controversial speeches. Malcolm X was murdered in New York City in 1965.

The Rural Life

For centuries, Nebraska was a rural wonderland. Images of the plains and hearty pioneers making houses out of sod are a key part of the state's history. In recent years, however, the state has witnessed a major shift. More and more Nebraskans have moved to urban and suburban centers in which to build their lives. As farms became larger and required fewer workers, small rural towns struggled to offer other well-paying jobs.

Slowly, communities became drained of their populations. People left in search of better-paying jobs elsewhere. It is a trend occurring across most of the Great Plains. The region has lost more than two-thirds of its population since the 1920s. Once-thriving communities are now practically boarded up, just one step away from becoming ghost towns. Nebraska now is home to seven of the twelve poorest counties in the United States.

Where did everybody go? With new industries and the rising cost of farming, parts of the rural Midwest are suffering from a population drain, as people move elsewhere in search of better opportunities. A once-thriving community, Orella is now a ghost town being slowly reclaimed by the prairie.

They are mostly large stretches of ranch lands, sprinkled with few people and even fewer towns.

Many Nebraskans are trying to find ways to prevent this from happening. One example is the town of Superior in southern Nebraska. The people of Superior know the hardship of losing factories and businesses

Many Nebraskans trace their roots to the land. The miles and miles of rolling plains gave rise to a state residents now cherish and work hard to improve.

and the important jobs they provide. So they have joined together, creating an economic development fund. A new office building has gone up on the edge of town. Some are hopeful these efforts will lead to a new life for the community. Others believe it is too little, too late. Only time will tell.

For now, most residents know that the times have changed and that their town must change with them. The people of Superior are looking for a balance, though, and seeking to hold on to their way of life. There are no easy solutions. In the meantime, like the people of many of the state's other rural towns, they are trying to come up with ways of coaxing tourists and new businesses to spend and invest money in their town. Still, for many of the people who stay in Nebraska's shrinking towns, the hard times have done little to lessen their love of the rural life. To them, it is the Nebraska they have always known and will always cherish.

Calendar of Events

Buffalo Commons Storytelling Festival

Top storytellers and musicians from across the state and the country gather each year in McCook. Cowboy poetry and ghost stories are just part of the fun at this event in early June.

Nebraskaland Days

The people of North Platte welcome folks from all over to their annual June festival featuring beauty contests, sports tournaments, parades, concerts, rodeos, arts and crafts, and all the food you can eat.

Cottonwood Prairie Festival

This outdoor festival comes to Hastings in June. It features the work of painters, sculptors, glassblowers, and jewelry makers.

Oregon Trail Days

Each July, Gering hosts this top frontier festival. Visitors enjoy cookoffs, square dancing, an art show, and one of the state's largest parades. For athletes, the event also features a bike race to the top of Scotts Bluff National Monument and a 5-mile run.

A rodeo

John C. Frémont Days

The people of Fremont gather together in July to celebrate the man who gave their town its name. Dancing, car shows, a reenactment of a frontier camp, and the exciting Roughstock Rodeo help to make this tribute complete.

Central Nebraska Ethnic Festival

Grand Island is the site of this cultural celebration kicking off in late July. Visitors are treated to Vietnamese dancers, Scottish pipers, and a wealth of ethnic and down-home foods and crafts sold from more than 100 booths.

Traditional Powwows

Nebraska's various native groups celebrate their culture and tradition at events across the state: Santee Sioux (June in Santee), Winnebago (July in Winnebago), Omaha Tribe's Harvest Celebration Powwow (first full-moon weekend in August in Macy), and Ponca (August in Niobrara).

Star City Holiday Festival

December in Lincoln means it is time for this long-running parade to once again take to the streets. Giant helium balloons, floats, and Santa Claus ring in the holiday season.

Homestead Days

4 How It Works

When it comes to their politics, Nebraskans are truly unique. They are the only people served by a state legislature that is unicameral. That means the body—or group—that makes state laws is made up of a one-part legislature. Most states have two-part legislatures, usually a senate and a house of representatives. For sixty-eight years, Nebraska followed this pattern as well. Then, in 1934, United States senator George W. Norris proposed a change. The idea was first suggested in 1915, but at that time it was struck down. Some felt it was not a good idea, but it was still debated and discussed in Nebraska for almost two decades. Norris helped to finally end the years of indecision. He proposed an amendment, or change, to the state constitution calling for the creation of the unicameral system.

The state has had five territorial capitols located in Omaha and three state capitols in Lincoln.

Those in favor of the plan believed it would make the lawmaking process simpler and more open to the public. They also argued that having a

Nebraska's capitol stands 400 feet high and is often called the Tower of the Plains. At the top of the capitol's dome is a statue known as the Sower. The 19-foot bronze sculpture is shown spreading seeds in a gesture of goodwill.

Branches of Government

Executive The governor is the head of the executive branch. He or she prepares the state budget and signs the laws that will best serve the state. A variety of other officials assist the governor. These include the lieutenant governor, secretary of state, attorney general, state treasurer, and auditor of public accounts. Each of these important positions, including the governor, is decided in a general election and carries a four-year term.

Legislative Nebraska is the only state with a unicameral system of government. That means the state legislature is made up of a single governing body, not two like the United States federal government and the other forty-nine states. Nebraska's legislature is made up of forty-nine voting members who do not identify or associate themselves with any specific political party. They each serve terms of four years.

Judicial The supreme court is the state's highest judicial body. The governor chooses the chief justice while the six other judges are selected from each of six districts in the state and serve six-year terms. The state is also served by lesser courts, including courts of appeals, twelve district courts, and courts that hear cases in each of the state's counties.

one-house system would save time and money. The new system would also change the way senators were elected. Candidates would not run as part of any official political party—such as democrat or republican. They would be judged as individuals and not as members of a larger political group. Voters would decide based on the strength of a candidate's ideas and record of service.

The voters were given the final say. In November 1934, they voted to adopt the change. The new unicameral legislature first met three years later in 1937. Norris's predictions turned out to be right. In the unicameral legislature's first year, legislative costs were chopped in half. The state's lawmakers and citizens were convinced they had made the right decision. The change shows the state was not afraid to take a bold step to fit its own unique needs.

All Kinds of Leaders

State officials are handed the tough task of running Nebraska. They create budgets and then decide how the state will spend its money on a variety of projects and programs. They also create the laws all Nebraskans must follow. These laws decide how fast you can drive on the state's roads and highways, how many days children go to school, and many other issues important to the daily lives of Nebraska's citizens. In a state with so many people, Nebraska's officials try to address the needs and concerns of all.

Most Nebraskans do not need to serve in the capitol in Lincoln in order to make a difference. There is plenty to be done in their own counties and communities. Nebraska's cities and towns are grouped together to form ninety-three counties. About two-thirds of these counties are run by a board of commissioners. Each board is typically made up of three to five members. Other counties are led by a seven-member board of supervisors. Board members oversee almost all aspects of county business. A variety of people help the board members in carrying out their duties. Clerks, treasurers, lawyers, police officers, and school superintendents are just some of the people who work hard to improve life in Nebraska's counties.

At a more local level, voters choose mayors or boards of commissioners to oversee the daily affairs in Nebraska's many cities, towns, and communities. These public servants play many different roles. They serve as lawmakers and managers. With more than 500 cities, towns, and villages, it takes a lot of people to make life in Nebraska run smoothly. They make sure the state's citizens have access to government-run services and programs. They also approve the funds for such important tasks as building and improving roads and buying new books for public libraries.

From Bill to Law

A bill is an idea for a new law. It can also suggest ways of changing laws that already exist. Bills are first introduced by a sponsor, usually a state senator. But sometimes the ideas for laws come straight from the people.

Once the senator has presented the bill, it is given a number by the clerk. The title of the bill is then read to the members of the legislature, after which it is sent to the reference committee. This is a group of nine senators who together form the executive board. They will move the bill along to what is known as a standing committee, a group of senators who will look more closely into the issues surrounding the bill. At the same time, the bill is published. Copies are made available to all senators as well as to the general public.

When the standing committee meets to discuss the bill, it holds a public hearing. This important step means the state senators hear from a variety of citizens. It gives Nebraskans a chance to come and express their opinions on issues that are important to them.

If the standing committee approves of the bill, it then goes to what is known as the general file. That is a daily list of bills the senators will be discussing and voting on. They consider all parts of the bill, including any amendments, or changes, the standing committee has made. Then it comes time to vote. If at least twenty-five state senators are in favor of the bill, it is reviewed to be sure it is in its proper form.

More changes can come at any time, which the legislature, again, must approve. The bill is then in its final form. Copies are once again sent to the senators. After the senators have been read the entire bill, they take the final vote. If the bill is approved, it is sent to the governor. The governor can sign the bill and make it an official part of state law. Or he or she can veto, or reject, the bill. If this happens, three-fifths, or at least thirty members, of the state legislature must still be in favor of the measure for it to become law. Once approved, the bill goes into effect in three months' time. It is then an official part of Nebraska state law.

If you would like to get in touch with Nebraska senators go to this Web site: http://www.unicam.state.ne.us/kids/senators.htm The senators are listed by their names and by the districts they represent. Ask a teacher, librarian, or parent to help you if you are not familiar with your district number.

5 Making a Living

Nebraska's greatest resources are its rich soils and plentiful water. Hardworking farmers have built Nebraska into one of the nation's leading farming states. The state's success has always been built on its crops and cattle. Through the twentieth century, the state's farms have changed, though. Fewer people now make a living directly from the land. The state's citizens have often been forced to change the way they make a living. New industries have emerged in the Cornhusker State. They offer Nebraskans more and different choices in the careers they pursue. While large combines and grain elevators are still a common sight in the state, so are businesses and factories that produce and sell an endless range of products.

Agriculture

From meat to beans to grains, many Nebraska products end up on America's dinner tables every day. But farming is not always an easy venture in the Cornhusker State. To encourage strong

A variety of Nebraska wildlife is featured in this popular—and monumental— display at Cabelas in Sidney, currently the state's top tourist attraction. The outdoor-supply store has added much to the state's wealth, providing many jobs and drawing shoppers and browsers from all around.

Currently 8.2 million acres of Nebraska farmland benefit from irrigation. The many dams built on the state's 24,000 miles of rivers and streams have helped this system become a success.

harvests, farmers have adopted a variety of soil- and water-saving methods through the years. They have led the way in the use of irrigation, crop rotation, and dry farming. Dry farming is a method used in very dry places. Crops that are resistant to drought are planted so that there is no need for irrigation.

The state's major crops include corn, soybeans, dry beans, wheat, hay, grain sorghum, potatoes, and sugar beets. Grapes, tomatoes, and orchard fruits are also grown from the land. The southwestern plateau is wheat country. Shimmering fields of the bristly grain wave in the wind, waiting for the harvest. Sugar beets and dry edible beans are another top crop grown there and in parts of the Panhandle as well. The state currently leads the nation in the amount of light red kidney beans and great northern beans it produces each year. In parts of the state where the soil is loose and sandy, many farmers have had success planting potatoes.

Cattle are raised in all of Nebraska's ninety-three counties. The Sandhills, in particular, are prime cattle country. Herds of Angus and Hereford cattle spend the spring and summer feasting on the abundant grasses. Nebraska currently leads the nation in the production of red meat. Though less valuable to the state's economy, hogs, dairy cattle, sheep, and chickens are raised as well. These operations are mostly found in the eastern part of the state, which supports a more diverse economy.

Nebraskans also raise and sell other meats, including bison, elk, ostrich, and fish.

Modern technology—in the form of all-terrain vehicles, or ATVs—makes a herder's tough job a little bit easier.

Recipe for Chocolate-Coated Popcorn Balls

Corn is an important crop on many Nebraska farms. Use this recipe to make a sweet treat out of tasty popcorn.

Ingredients:

8 cups of popcorn (popped and ready to eat)
1/2 cup granulated sugar
1/2 cup corn syrup
1/4 cup butter or margarine
2 tablespoons cocoa powder (unsweetened)
1/2 cup chopped peanuts
1 cup mini-marshmallows

Have an adult help you combine the sugar, corn syrup, butter, and cocoa in a medium-sized pan. Carefully stir these ingredients over a low heat on the stove and bring the mixture slowly to a boil. Make sure the ingredients do not get too hot or they will stick to the bottom of the pan. Once bubbles appear, turn off the heat and remove the pan from the stove. All the ingredients in the pan should be melted and look like a slightly gooey sauce.

Next, have an adult help you pour this mixture over the popcorn. One person can pour the sauce while the other person stirs the popcorn. Add the peanuts and the marshmallows and stir again until everything is coated in the chocolate sauce.

Wait until this mixture has cooled enough so that it will not burn your hands. Wash your hands, coat your fingers with some butter, and shape the chocolate popcorn mixture into balls about the size of tennis balls.

Let the popcorn balls cool and then enjoy!

NOTE: This recipe makes about 18 popcorn balls

Mineral Wealth

Nebraska is not known for its mining industry. Still, plenty of mineral wealth lies locked beneath its soils. Oil and natural gas are found in the Panhandle, mostly in Kimball and Cheyenne counties. Oil was first discovered in the state in 1939. By the early 1940s, several companies had begun drilling, and in no time, oil had become the state's most valuable mineral resource.

Sand and gravel are major state products as well. Large quantities are gathered from across the state but mostly along the Republican and Platte River valleys. Once collected, they are used mostly in concrete and for the surfaces of roads. Similarly, stone is plentiful in the state, mostly in the southern and eastern regions.

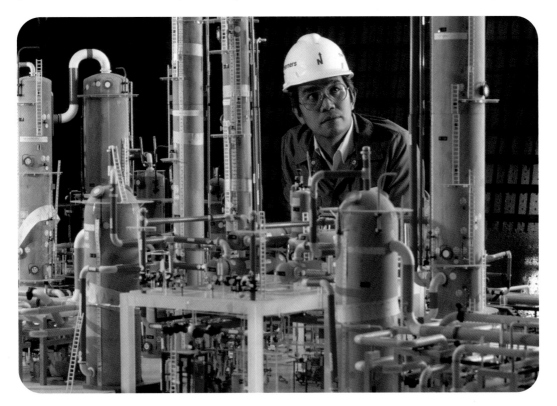

A worker in Omaha inspects a model for a proposed oil refinery.

Limestone, sandstone, chalkrock, and smaller amounts of quartzite are also used in road building and in the creation of cement. Limestone quarries are found along the Missouri River in the state's southeastern stretch. Clay, needed mostly in making tiles and bricks, is another treasure offered up from the Nebraska countryside. It is found across the state and is a major part of the soil of the badlands.

Manufacturing, Services, and Retail

Nebraskans make and manufacture a variety of items. Clocks, magnets, furniture, fans, golf clubs, and pipe organs are just some of the things produced in the state. Workers also produce large-scale items in some of the state's major factories. The creation of machinery, farm equipment, and car parts helps keep people working and on the go. The state's farmers need to be able to plant and harvest their crops. Truck drivers, too, must be able to transport farm products to processing centers across the state. So it is not surprising a successful industry has emerged in the state by supplying workers with these items.

Since Nebraska is such a major agricultural state, food processing is also big business. Currently the processing and creation of food products is the state's largest source of income. Dairy items, meats, and flour and flour-based products such as cereals and pasta are just some of the foods that are prepared in the Cornhusker State. Workers also process grain to feed to the state's large herds of livestock. Meat packing is also a major industry.

These various business operations can be found across the state. But the state's largest economic center is Omaha. Slowly through the years, the city has emerged as a major business

In an Omaha laboratory, two technicians study seedlings in an attempt to learn how the state's fields and farms can become more productive.

center. Food processing, insurance, telecommunications, and health care are just some of the major industries that keep Omahans busy.

Lincoln is another business center. In addition to the University of Nebraska, which employs thousands of people, the state capital hosts a wealth of companies that produce, among other things, medicine and related medical products, and transportation parts and equipment. Insurance and telecommunications are important Lincoln industries as well.

Mutual of Omaha is one of America's best-known insurance companies. But it is certainly not the only one that makes its home in Nebraska. Omaha is home to many companies selling policies that cover people's health, homes, cars, and lives.

Products & Resources

Sorghum

Sorghum is one of the state's main grain crops, grown mostly in the southeastern and south-central portions. It is used mostly as feed for cattle, hogs, and chickens. It is well-suited to the Nebraska climate and is able to thrive in areas with high heat and little water. The head of the plant sports hundreds of "berries" and can be red, white, bronze, or yellowish.

Machinery and Transportation Equipment

Farmers and ranchers need a lot of equipment—tractors, grain elevators, and combines, just to name a few. Nebraska's workers also produce equipment for tractor trailers, trucks, and other giants of the road.

Popcorn

Popcorn is big business in the Cornhusker State. Whether it is yellow, white, or mushroom popcorn, companies in Chapman, Clearwater, Schuyler, Hastings, North Loup, and Phillips keep snackers happy and coming back for more.

Dry Edible Beans

Nebraska is the country's top producer of these tiny legumes. Kidney beans, great northern beans, and pinto beans help to keep the nation—and the world—well fed.

Steaks and Other Meats

Which is your favorite—sirloin, rib eye, or filet mignon? Whatever your preference, Nebraska businesses offer the perfect cut. From raising the livestock to processing the meat, Nebraska ranches and packaging plants bring money to the state. If Spam or other processed meats are more to your liking, a Hormel meat-packing plant is located in Fremont.

Winter Wheat

In 2003, the state harvested and sold 83 million bushels of this important grain. That earned Nebraska the top spot in winter-wheat production. The crops are processed and find their way into the foods we eat every day, including breads, pasta, and cereal.

It takes a wide range of Nebraskans to keep the state productive and strong. Doctors, mechanics, cooks, librarians, and real estate agents are just some of the many roles state residents fill in order to serve and assist their fellow Nebraskans. To many of the state's citizens, the pioneer spirit is still alive, and helping each other out is not an old-fashioned notion. Though the state has changed much from the days Native Americans freely roamed the plains, Nebraskans know that whatever challenges the future will bring, they will face them together.

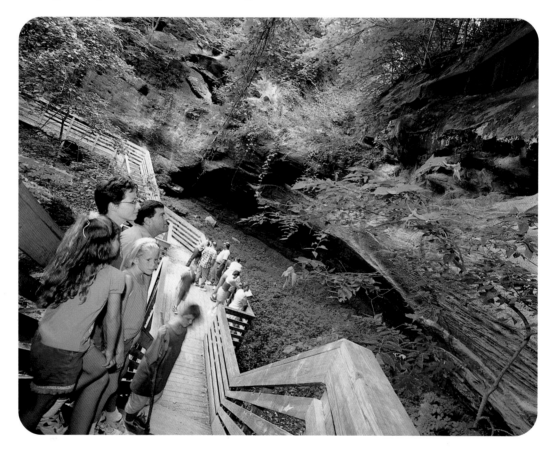

Nature lovers gather along the boardwalk at Indian Cave Park. Tourism is a major money earner for the Cornhusker State. For some state residents, Nebraska is a secret that is best kept. For others, the state's often unexpected beauty is a treasure waiting to be discovered.

Nebraska was one of the last states to adopt its own official flag. In 1925, lawmakers set out to change that, adopting a banner that consisted of "a reproduction of the Great Seal of the State charged on the center in gold and silver on a field of national blue." Although it was technically adopted in that year, at the time this important symbol was called the state banner and not named Nebraska's official flag until 1965.

During a special session of the state legislature, called in 1867, one of the bills lawmakers adopted called for the creation of the state seal. It would show "a steamboat ascending the Missouri River, the mechanic arts . . . represented by a smith with a hammer and anvil, in the foreground, agriculture to be represented by a settlers cabin, sheaves of wheat, and stalks of growing corn, in the background a train of cars heading towards the Rocky Mountains, and on the extreme west, the Rocky Mountains to be plainly in view [and] around the top of the circle, to be in capital letters, the motto: 'Equality Before the Law.'" Finally, circling the seal are the words Great Seal of the State of Nebraska March 1, 1867.

NEBRASKA

Legend:
- ★ State Capital
- ⬠ City or Town
- ● City or Town
- Interstate Highway
- U.S. Highway
- State Highway
- National Forest
- National Monument
- National Monument
- Indian Reservation
- Wildlife Refuge
- State Park
- Highest Point in the State
- ☆ Historic Site

miles
0
30

Oglala National Grassland
Toadstool Geologic Park
Agate Fossil Beds National Monument
Horse Creek Treaty Grounds
Scotts Bluff National Monument
Chimney Rock National Historic Site
Gering
Scottsbluff
Bushnell
Panorama Point
Sidney
North Platte River
South Platte River
Alliance
Crescent Lake National Wildlife Refuge
Sand Hill Region
Chadron
Nebraska National Forest
Niobrara River
Hyannis
Merritt Reservoir
Samuel R. McKelvie National Forest
Valentine National Wildlife Refuge
Moon Lake
Valentine
Fort Niobrara National Wildlife Refuge
Ogallala
North Platte
Nebraska National Forest
Calamus River
O'Neill
Niobrara River
Ashfall Fossil Beds State Historic Park
Santee Reservation
McCook
Broken Bow
Calamus Reservoir
Bartlett
Elkhorn River
Gothenburg
Lexington
Kearney
Platte River
Holdrege
Harlan County Lake
Republican River
Columbus
Norfolk
Wayne
Winnebago Reservation
Omaha Reservation
Hastings
Grand Island
Aurora
York
Seward
Schuyler
Wahoo
Fremont
South Sioux City
Fairbury
Homestead National Monument of America
Beatrice
Lincoln
Papillion
Bellevue
Plattsmouth
Omaha
Missouri River
Falls City
Nebraska City
Indian Cave State Park
Sac and Fox Reservation

Highways (shields):
20, 71, 385, 26, 61, 2, 83, 81, 6, 34, 136, 77, 92, 22, 281, 275, 12

Beautiful Nebraska

Words by James Fras and Guy Gage Miller
Music by James Fras

Beau - ti - ful Ne - bra - ska, peace-ful prai - rie land. Laced with ma - ny ri - vers

and the hills of sand: Dark green val - leys cra-dled in the earth. Rain and sun - shine

bring a-bun-dant birth. Beau-ti - ful Ne-bra - ska, as you look a - round, You will find a rain - bow

reach-ing to the ground: All these won - ders by the Mas-ter's hand: Beau-ti - ful Ne-bra - ska

land. We are so proud of this state where we

live. There is no place that has so much to give.

Beau-ti - ful Ne-bra - ska, as you look a - round, you will find a rain - bow reach-ing to the ground:

All these won - ders by the Mas-ter's hand. Beau-ti - ful Ne-bra - ska land.

State Song

More About Nebraska

Books

American World and Geographic Publishing. *Nebraska: A Photographic Celebration*. Helena, Montana: Farcountry Press, 1993.

Broida, Marian. *Hands-on History: Projects about Westward Expansion*. New York: Marshall Cavendish Benchmark, 2004.

Opat, Jamie Stockman. *Uniquely Nebraska*. Chicago: Heinneman Library, 2004.

Web Sites

Nebraska for Kids
http://www.visitnebraska.org/about/kids

Nebraska State Historical Society-Kids! Stuff
http://www.nebraskahistory.org/oversite/kidstuff

Nebraska Wildlife Federation
http://www.nebraskawildlife.org

Official Web Site of Nebraska
http://www.nebraska.gov/index.phtml

About the Author

Doug Sanders lives in New York. One of his favorite vacations was spent in the Panhandle of Nebraska. Highlights included visits to Toadstool Geologic Park, Fort Robinson, and Agate Fossil Beds National Monument.

Index

Page numbers in **boldface** are illustrations.